W9-BDK-994

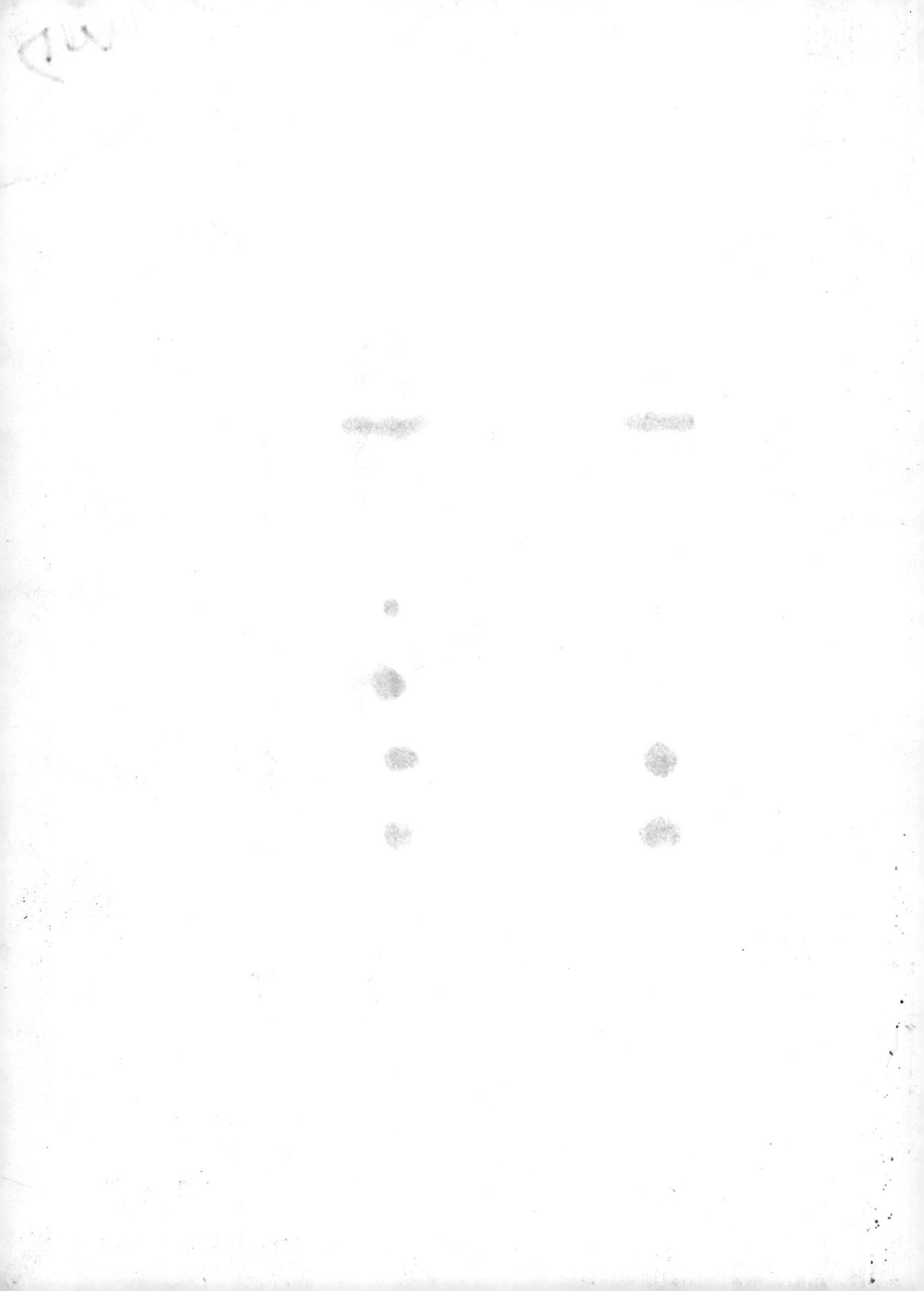

Entertainment

MOVIE BLOCKBUSTERS

By Mark Stewart

Gareth Stevens Publishing

Please visit our web site at www.garethstevens.com.
For a free catalog describing Gareth Stevens Publishing's list of high-quality books, call 1-800-542-2595 (USA) or 1-800-387-3178 (Canada). Gareth Stevens Publishing's fax: 1-877-542-2596

Library of Congress Cataloging-in-Publication Data
Stewart, Mark, 1960–
Movie blockbusters / by Mark Stewart.
p. cm. — (Ultimate 10: entertainment)
Includes bibliographical references and index.
ISBN-10: 0-8368-9163-5 ISBN-13: 978-0-8368-9163-8 (lib. bdg.)
ISBN-10: 1-4339-2211-8 ISBN-13: 978-1-4339-2211-4 (softcover)
1. Blockbusters (Motion pictures)—Juvenile literature. I. Title.
PN1995.9.B598S74 2009
791.43'75—dc22 2009010533

This edition first published in 2010 by
Gareth Stevens Publishing
A Weekly Reader® Company
1 Reader's Digest Road
Pleasantville, NY 10570-7000 USA

Executive Managing Editor: Lisa M. Herrington
Senior Designer: Keith Plechaty

Produced by Editorial Directions, Inc.

Art Direction and Page Production: The Design Lab

Picture credits
Cover: (tl) PaulPaladin/Shutterstock, (cl) ©Everett Collection, (bl) ©New Line/Courtesy Everett Collection, (cr) ©Walt Disney/Courtesy Everett Collection, (b) Valery Potapova/Shutterstock; title page, (l) ©Everett Collection, (c) ©New Line/Courtesy Everett Collection, (r) ©Walt Disney/Courtesy Everett Collection, (b) Valery Potapova/Shutterstock; cover, title page: sabri deniz kizil/Shutterstock; pp. 4–5, 11: ©TM and Copyright ©20th Century Fox Film Corp; pp. 6, 10, 14, 18, 22, 26, 30, 34, 38, 42: PaulPaladin/Shutterstock; p. 7: ©Photos 12/Alamy; p. 8: (t) Steve Granitz/WireImage, (b) ©Roger Ressmeyer/CORBIS; p. 9: ©Douglas Kirkland/CORBIS; p. 12: ©TM and Copyright ©20th Century Fox Film Corp. All rights reserved. Courtesy: Everett Collection.; p. 13: ©TM and Copyright ©20th Century Fox Film Corp. All rights reserved. Courtesy: Everett Collection.; p. 15: ©Everett Collection; p. 16: (t) ©Everett Collection, (b) Silver Screen Collection/ Hulton Archive/Getty Images; p. 17: ©Sunset Boulevard/Corbis; p. 19 ©CinemaPhoto/Corbis; p. 20 GAB Archive/Redferns; p. 21 ©Bettmann/CORBIS; p. 23: ©Warner Brothers/Courtesy Everett Collection; p. 24: (t) ©Everett Collection, (b): AP Photo/Kirsty Wigglesworth; p. 25: ©Warner Bros./Courtesy Everett Collection; p. 27: ©Everett Collection; p. 28: (t) ©Everett Collection, (b) ©New Line/Courtesy Everett Collection; p. 29: ©New Line/Courtesy Everett Collection; p. 31: ©Everett Collection; p. 32: ©Everett Collection; p. 33: ©Everett Collection; p. 35: ©Everett Collection; p. 36: ©Buena Vista Pictures/Courtesy Everett Collection; p. 37: ©Walt Disney Co./Courtesy: Everett Collection; p. 39: ©Columbia Pictures/Courtesy Everett Collection; p. 40: ©Melissa Moseley/Sony Pictures/Bureau L.A. Collection/Corbis; p. 41: ©Columbia/Courtesy Everett Collection; p. 43: ©Walt Disney/Courtesy Everett Collection; p. 44: (t) ©Walt Disney/Courtesy Everett Collection, (b) AP Photo/Library of Congress; p. 45: ©Walt Disney/Courtesy Everett Collection; p. 46: (t) ©Everett Collection, (b) ©Peter Mountain/Industrial Light & Magic/Bureau L.A. Collection/Corbis

Printed in the United States of America

1 2 3 4 5 6 7 8 9 14 13 12 11 10 09

TABLE OF CONTENTS

Words in the glossary appear in **bold** type the first time they are used in the text.

Welcome to The Ultimate 10! This exciting series highlights the very best from the world of entertainment.

When a movie takes in more money than it cost to make, it is a success. When millions of people around the country see it, and everyone is talking about it, it has become a blockbuster. Just about any type of movie can become a blockbuster.

Audiences were on the edge of their seats as *Titanic* survivors rowed away from the sinking ship.

All blockbusters have something in common, however. They capture the audience's imagination, and people want to watch these films over and over.

This book tells the stories of 10 "ultimate" movie blockbusters. Learn what it takes to make a megahit. Get the behind-the-scenes stories of some of the most famous films in history. You may never watch a movie the same way again.

Mighty Movies

Here are 10 of the greatest blockbusters of all time.

Star Wars

Titanic

The Wizard of Oz

The Sound of Music

Harry Potter and the Sorcerer's Stone

The Lord of the Rings: The Fellowship of the Ring

Jaws

The Lion King

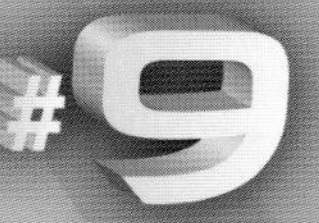

Spider-Man

Finding Nemo

Star Wars

A long time ago in a galaxy far, far away ... From the moment that famous phrase rolled onto big screens in 1977, audiences knew they were in for something they had never seen before. *Star Wars* was followed by five more movies that earned more than $4 billion in ticket sales—and billions more in merchandise. The story was classic—the triumph of good over evil. Memorable heroes, lovable droids, and one of scariest villains in movie history helped make *Star Wars* a smashing success.

Roll Credits

Film: *Star Wars*
Year: 1977
Studio: Twentieth Century–Fox
Director: George Lucas
Stars: Mark Hamill (Luke Skywalker), Harrison Ford (Han Solo), Carrie Fisher (Princess Leia), Alec Guinness (Obi-Wan Kenobi)
Oscar nominations: 11
Oscar wins: 6

Hot Shot

George Lucas was the hottest director in Hollywood in the mid-1970s. He had just directed the box-office smash *American Graffiti*. He was being offered serious movies. For his next film, Lucas wanted to create a science-fiction fantasy set in space. Many people thought he was joking. Some major studios passed on his idea.

Star Wars was no joke to Lucas. His plan was to tell a classic tale using the latest special effects. Lucas wanted to make an exciting, feel-good movie that kids and adults would want to see again and again. *Star Wars* tells the story of a group of rebels who are battling an evil empire. An elderly Jedi knight teaches young Luke Skywalker about an energy field called the Force. The powers of the Force help Luke fight the empire.

CLASSIC QUOTE

"May the Force be with you."

—Han Solo to Luke Skywalker before the film's final battle

Luke Skywalker, Princess Leia, and Han Solo battle the evil empire.

Word of Mouth

During filming, many members of the cast and crew thought *Star Wars* would be a flop. The film went over its **budget**, and its release was delayed by several months.

Star Wars finally reached theaters in late May 1977. The film was a smash hit. By the end of the summer, *Star Wars* had earned more than $300 million worldwide. It was the first film ever to take in that much.

Soon fans were buying *Star Wars* action figures, comics, and lunch boxes. The money Lucas made from *Star Wars* merchandise enabled him to make the **sequel**, *The Empire Strikes Back*, with his own money.

The robots C-3PO and R2-D2 bring comic relief to the movie.

FOR THE RECORD

In all, six live-action *Star Wars* movies reached the big screen. The original movie turned out to be episode four of the story. Here is how they fit together:

Episode	Title	Premiere
I	*The Phantom Menace*	1999
II	*Attack of the Clones*	2002
III	*Revenge of the Sith*	2005
IV	*Star Wars (A New Hope)*	1977
V	*The Empire Strikes Back*	1980
VI	*Return of the Jedi*	1983

An artist works on a model of the Rancor monster from *Return of the Jedi*. Many talented people worked to create the groundbreaking special effects and creatures in *Star Wars*.

Light and Magic

Star Wars caught moviegoers by surprise. There was not a lot of publicity before it opened. People were astounded by the special effects. Lucas had made the thrilling space battles and strange creatures seem real.

Lucas had started his own company, Industrial Light & Magic, to create the groundbreaking special effects. Industrial Light & Magic has since created effects for many films. Its computer-generated "stars" have appeared in *Jurassic Park*, *The Mask*, *Hulk*, the *Pirates of the Caribbean* movies, and *Transformers*.

DID YOU KNOW?

Two actors created the great villain Darth Vader. Bodybuilder David Prowse, who stands 6 feet 7 inches (201 centimeters) tall, wore Vader's costume. James Earl Jones provided Vader's deep voice.

#2 Titanic

When the RMS *Titanic* sank after hitting an iceberg in 1912, it became the world's most famous disaster. Who could have imagined that *Titanic* would become the world's biggest box-office success—85 years later? Director James Cameron did. To tell his story, Cameron mixed real and computerized sets. He also mixed real and fictional characters. Audiences could not take their eyes off the screen. *Titanic* remains the biggest moneymaker in movie history.

Roll Credits

Film: *Titanic*
Year: 1997
Studios: Paramount and 20th Century Fox
Director: James Cameron
Stars: Leonardo DiCaprio (Jack Dawson), Kate Winslet (Rose Calvert), Billy Zane (Cal Hockley)
Oscar nominations: 14
Oscar wins: 11

The scenes of the *Titanic* sinking are some of the most expensive—and memorable—in movie history.

The Big Ship

For most of his life, Cameron had been fascinated by the story of the *Titanic*. More than 1,500 people died in the disaster. Still, Cameron felt it was a story of life, not death. He wanted to show this through the story of Jack and Rose. They meet on the ship and fall in love. Cameron selected Leonardo DiCaprio and Kate Winslet to play these roles.

A full-scale model of the ship was built. It sat in a 17 million–gallon (64 million–liter) tank for the film. A special lift sat below the water to tilt the model during the terrifying sinking scenes. Cameron also shot **footage** of the actual *Titanic* for the movie. It lay 2 miles (3.2 kilometers) below the Atlantic Ocean's surface.

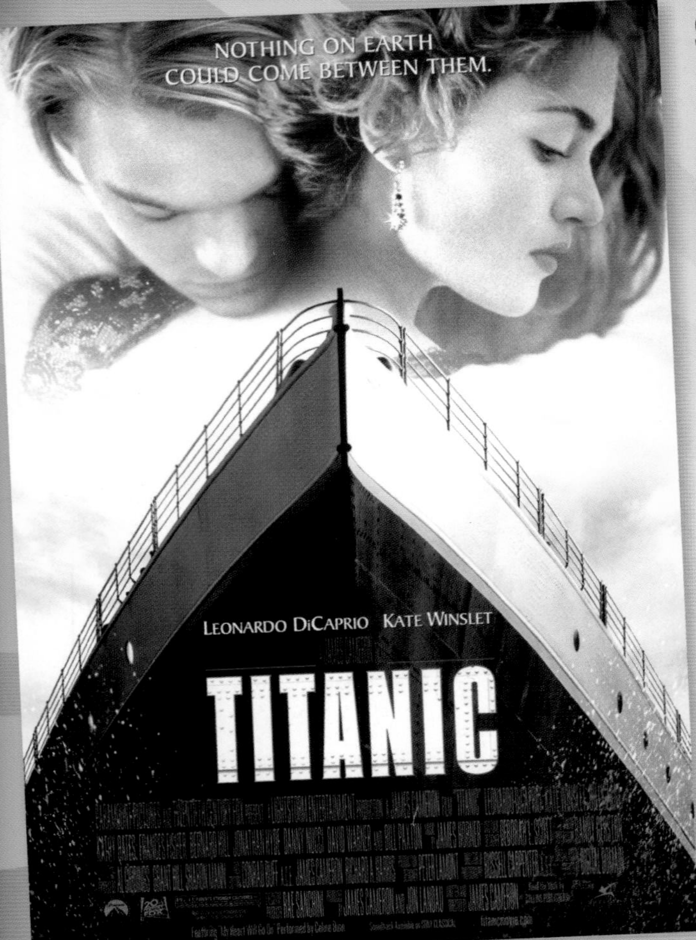

Titanic took in more than $600 million in ticket sales in the United States.

Solid Start

The stakes were high for *Titanic* when it opened in December 1997. Cameron had insisted on getting every detail right. This sent the cost of the film over $200 million. It also delayed the opening by several months. The two studios paying for the movie nearly ran out of money.

Titanic's first weekend was great. It made nearly $30 million in three days in the United States alone. As word spread about the movie, theaters began to sell out. *Titanic* stayed in theaters until fall 1998. It was the first movie ever to earn more than $1 billion worldwide.

FOR THE RECORD

Titanic was nominated for 14 **Academy Awards**, or Oscars. Only *All About Eve*, a 1957 drama about an aging actress, has received as many Oscar nominations. Nine other movies, including such big hits as *Mary Poppins*, *Forrest Gump*, and *Gone With the Wind*, have received 13 nominations.

Award Winner

Titanic was more than a financial success. It tied a record by winning 11 Oscars. The blend of great storytelling, great acting, and great filmmaking inspired a whole generation of young actors and directors. Even the theme song, "My Heart Will Go On," sung by Celine Dion, was a number-one hit!

Leonardo DiCaprio and Kate Winslet were nominated for Academy Awards for their roles. Thanks to the success of *Titanic*, they were offered more roles that helped them showcase their talent. In 2009, Winslet won the Academy Award for best actress in *The Reader*.

The love story between Jack and Rose is at the heart of *Titanic*.

CLASSIC QUOTE

"I'm the king of the world!"

—Jack Dawson

DID YOU KNOW?

Gloria Stuart played Rose as an old woman. She had made her first movie in 1932. At age 87, Stuart became the oldest actress ever nominated for an Academy Award.

#3 The Wizard of Oz

During the Great Depression of the 1930s, many people lost their jobs. To forget their troubles, Americans flocked to movie theaters. *The Wizard of Oz* is one of the best-loved films from this time. It tells the story of Dorothy Gale, a girl who wakes up after a tornado in the magical land of Oz. There, she meets unforgettable friends and an evil witch as she searches for a way back home. The story is as fresh and original today as it was when it first blazed across the screen.

Roll Credits

Film: *The Wizard of Oz* **Year:** 1939
Studio: Metro Goldwyn Mayer (MGM)
Directors: Victor Fleming and King Vidor
Stars: Judy Garland (Dorothy), Frank Morgan (the Wizard), Ray Bolger (the Scarecrow), Bert Lahr (the Cowardly Lion), Jack Haley (the Tin Man), Billie Burke (Glinda the Good Witch of the North), Margaret Hamilton (the Wicked Witch)
Oscar nominations: 4 **Oscar wins:** 2

Casting Call

Casting the different roles in *The Wizard of Oz* was difficult. Many people expected Shirley Temple, a famous child star, to play Dorothy. But her singing style was not right for songs like "Over the Rainbow." Instead, 16-year-old Judy Garland was chosen.

CLASSIC QUOTE
"Toto, I have a feeling we're not in Kansas anymore."
—Dorothy Gale

Two popular dancers were hired to play important parts. Buddy Ebsen was going to play the Scarecrow, and Ray Bolger was cast as the Tin Man. Bolger convinced the **producer** that he and Ebsen should switch roles. Ebsen agreed to play the Tin Man. The Tin Man's silver makeup made him sick, however, and he left the film. Jack Haley, a well-known stage actor, was hired to fill in.

The Wizard of Oz features some of the most memorable characters in movie history.

Dorothy and her friends travel down the Yellow Brick Road to Emerald City. That is where the Wizard of Oz lives.

On the Screen

The Wizard of Oz was magical. People loved how it starts in black and white and becomes color when Dorothy enters the Land of Oz. Its songs became classics. "Over the Rainbow" won the Oscar for best song.

The elaborate sets and switch to color drove the movie's cost up to about $3 million. During its first run, the movie took in about $3 million. Only later did it become a blockbuster. *The Wizard of Oz* was released in theaters several times in later years. Starting in the 1950s, the movie found a new life on TV. It was aired as a once-a-year special until 1991. Each year, the movie gained even more young fans.

FOR THE RECORD

In *The Wizard of Oz*, Margaret Hamilton created one of the greatest movie villains of all time. The green-faced Wicked Witch of the West terrified audiences from the moment she swooped in on her broom. Her threat to Dorothy is legendary: "I'll get you, my pretty, and your little dog, too!" The filmmakers actually cut some of the Wicked Witch's lines so kids wouldn't become too scared.

Oz and Beyond

The Wizard of Oz made Judy Garland a superstar. She won a special Academy Award for young actors for playing Dorothy. She would later win another Oscar, for the 1954 film *A Star Is Born.*

The Wizard of Oz has had an impact on TV and the theater. During the 1960s, many families bought color TVs so they could watch the moment when Dorothy steps into the Land of Oz and the film changes from black and white to glorious color. In 2003, the musical *Wicked* **premiered** on Broadway. It tells the story of the Wicked Witch of the West. *Wicked* became one of the most popular plays ever.

Dorothy's dog, Toto, is one of the most famous movie pets of all time.

DID YOU KNOW?

The movie was based on a novel by L. Frank Baum called *The Wonderful Wizard of Oz*, which was published in 1900. The book and the movie are similar, but there is one key difference. Dorothy's silver slippers in the book became ruby red in the movie!

The Sound of Music

The power and beauty of song can lift the human spirit. In *The Sound of Music*, a young nanny named Maria cares for the seven von Trapp children. Maria brings music and love into the lives of the children and their strict father. The movie blends wonderful music and humor with breathtaking scenery. This combination helped make *The Sound of Music* one of the most popular movie musicals of all time.

Roll Credits

Film: *The Sound of Music*
Year: 1965
Studio: Twentieth Century–Fox
Director: Robert Wise
Stars: Julie Andrews (Maria), Christopher Plummer (Captain von Trapp)
Oscar nominations: 10
Oscar wins: 5

From Stage to Screen

The Sound of Music is based on the real-life story of Maria von Trapp. She had studied to become a nun. She left the convent to care for the von Trapp children after their mother died. Maria later married Captain von Trapp. The family fled their home in Austria near the start of World War II.

Maria's story was first turned into a hit Broadway musical. Mary Martin starred in the play when it opened in 1959. The success of the play led to the movie version. Julie Andrews landed the lead role in the film. She had won an Oscar for her role as the magical nanny in *Mary Poppins*.

CLASSIC QUOTE

"I can't seem to stop singing wherever I am."
—Maria

The movie opens with Julie Andrews singing the song "The Sound of Music." Much of the movie was shot in and around Salzburg, Austria, where the von Trapps once lived.

Feeling the Love

The Sound of Music premiered in March 1965. Most **critics** gave it good reviews. The public fell in love with the film. Many people went to see it over and over. *The Sound of Music* made more than $150 million for the movie studio. That broke the all-time box-office record in the United States.

The success of *The Sound of Music* had a huge impact on the movie business. In 1965, Twentieth Century–Fox was in danger of going out of business. It had lost millions making the movie *Cleopatra* in 1963. *The Sound of Music* enabled the studio to keep making great movies.

The Sound of Music set box office records and helped save Twentieth Century–Fox.

FOR THE RECORD

The legendary team of Richard Rodgers and Oscar Hammerstein wrote the music and lyrics for the film. Its famous songs include "My Favorite Things" and "Do-Re-Mi." Rodgers and Hammerstein had also written such classic musicals as *Oklahoma!* and *The King and I*. *The Sound of Music* was their last **score**. Hammerstein passed away after the play opened on Broadway.

The cast of *The Sound of Music* sings "So Long, Farewell."

High Notes

The Sound of Music was nominated for 10 Oscars. It won five, including best picture and best score. The songs in *The Sound of Music* became remarkably popular. The **soundtrack** album has sold more than 10 million copies.

Julie Andrews was already a star when she made *The Sound of Music.* However, the movie gave her the most memorable role of her career.

> **"There's a reason this musical has won the hearts of so many: because it's a great movie all around, but more than that, watching it just makes you feel wonderful."**
>
> **—David Cornelius, eFilmCritic.com**

DID YOU KNOW?

In the film's opening scene, the camera flies through a valley and swoops in on Maria. To get the shot, the camera was mounted on a helicopter. Wind from the helicopter kept knocking Julie Andrews over.

Harry Potter and the Sorcerer's Stone

Turning a great book into a great movie is always a big challenge. Imagine trying to do that with one of the most popular books of all time. By 2000, millions of readers had already fallen in love with *Harry Potter and the Sorcerer's Stone*. They knew J. K. Rowling's story of a young wizard's struggle against evil inside and out. How would fans react to seeing Harry's adventures at Hogwarts on the big screen?

Roll Credits

Film: *Harry Potter and the Sorcerer's Stone*
Year: 2001
Studio: Warner Bros.
Director: Chris Columbus
Stars: Daniel Radcliffe (Harry Potter), Rupert Grint (Ron Weasley), Emma Watson (Hermione Granger), Robbie Coltrane (Rubeus Hagrid), Richard Harris (Albus Dumbledore), Alan Rickman (Severus Snape)
Oscar nominations: 3 **Oscar wins:** 0

Getting Started

When the first Harry Potter book was published in 1997, it quickly became a sensation. Even kids who don't normally like to read got caught up in the story of a boy who goes to wizard school. Starting in the late 1990s, several Hollywood studios tried to buy the **rights** to the Harry Potter series. J. K. Rowling was very stubb orn. She did not want anything in the bo oks changed. She also insisted on using British actors.

Rowling agreed to work wi
Chris Columbus and s ith director
Kloves. Work begar creenwriter Steve
of children tried n in 2000. Thousands
and his friends out for the parts of Harry
Daniel Radc s Hermione and Ron.
He and t cliffe was cast as Harry.
the m the other child actors in
ovie were all unknowns.

CLASSIC QUOTE

"There is no good and evil, there is only power, and those too weak to seek it."

—Harry's enemy, Lord Voldemort

Daniel Radcliffe (middle) was 11 years old when he was chosen to play Harry Potter.

The students' flying lessons is one of the most memorable scenes in the movie.

Solid Start

Harry Potter fans had very high expectations for the movie, and they weren't disappointed. All the fabulous characters and creatures and the magic of Hogwarts School of Witchcraft and Wizardry came alive on the big screen. The movie made more than $90 million its first weekend. People went back to see it again and again. By the time *Harry Potter and the Sorcerer's Stone* left theaters, it had made $974 million worldwide.

FOR THE RECORD

J. K. Rowling came up with the idea for Harry Potter while riding a train across England. She began spending her days in cafés, writing the adventures of Harry Potter. She based the character Hermione on herself at age 11. Today, Rowling is one of the world's most successful authors. Her seven Harry Potter books have sold more than 400 million copies.

Super Sequels

Harry Potter and the Sorcerer's Stone was the first of a series of Harry Potter movies. The first sequel was *Harry Potter and the Chamber of Secrets*, which was released in 2002. As with the books, each movie tells the story of another year at Hogwarts. With each new adventure, Harry and his friends are a year older and face more serious dangers.

Every Harry Potter film became a huge hit. By the end of 2008, the series had made almost $4.5 billion. By the time the last film is released, that total could be more than $7 billion.

Harry, Ron, and Hermione look out for dementors in *Harry Potter and the Order of the Phoenix.*

DID YOU KNOW?

J. K. Rowling's first book was called *Harry Potter and the Philosopher's Stone.* Its title was changed to *Harry Potter and the Sorcerer's Stone* for sale in the United States.

The Lord of the Rings: The Fellowship of the Ring

In the Lord of the Rings books, J. R. R. Tolkien created a world called Middle-Earth. Tolkien fans long imagined what this world looked like. They found out in 2001 when *The Fellowship of the Ring* became one of the biggest blockbusters in history.

ROLL CREDITS

Film: *The Lord of the Rings: The Fellowship of the Ring*
Year: 2001
Studio: New Line Cinema
Director: Peter Jackson
Stars: Elijah Wood (Frodo), Sean Astin (Sam), Ian McKellen (Gandalf), Orlando Bloom (Legolas), Viggo Mortensen (Aragorn), Liv Tyler (Arwen), Cate Blanchett (Galadriel), Christopher Lee (Saruman), John Rhys-Davies (Gimli)
Oscar nominations: 13
Oscar wins: 4

In *The Fellowship of the Ring*, Frodo Baggins (front) and the other Hobbits begin the long trip to Mount Doom.

Casting Call

CLASSIC QUOTE

"I know what I must do, it's just that ... I'm afraid to do it."

—Frodo Baggins, on his journey to return the ring to Mount Doom

In *The Fellowship of the Ring*, the fate of Middle-Earth rests in the hands of young Frodo Baggins. Frodo and his companions must fight their way to Mount Doom and destroy the ring he possesses.

Director Peter Jackson brought the actors together in New Zealand six weeks before filming began. They learned sword-fighting, horsemanship, and how to pronounce the difficult words in Tolkien's story.

Meanwhile, the special effects crew was hard at work. They had to create the sets for Middle-Earth. They used computers to design the terrifying creatures that lived there. The price tag for the movie reached $94 million.

Holiday Treat

The Fellowship of the Ring opened just before Christmas in 2001. Fans of Tolkien's books had waited decades to see the story on the big screen. They had seen trailers for the movie earlier that year. It looked spectacular. But no one was prepared for the incredible special effects, horrifying monsters, and huge battle scenes. The movie was a smash hit.

Movie critics gave *The Fellowship of the Ring* a thumbs-up. They praised the acting, camerawork, and musical score. Two months later, the film won four Academy Awards—for makeup, visual effects, music, and **cinematography**.

Ian McKellen played the wizard Gandalf.

FOR THE RECORD

One of the most fantastic characters in *The Lord of the Rings* is Gollum. Gollum is played by Andy Serkis, but audiences never see the actor. Instead they see a creature that is hundreds of years old. Gollum was created with **computer-generated imagery (CGI)**. Serkis performed Gollum's cat-like movements and his weird voice. This footage was then mixed with computer images of Gollum made by artists and **animators**. The final result is so realistic that it is easy to forget Gollum was created by a computer.

Viggo Mortensen stars as Aragorn in *The Lord of the Rings: The Return of the King*. The movie won 11 Academy Awards.

First of the Three

The Fellowship of the Ring was followed by *The Two Towers* (2002) and *The Return of the King* (2003). The three films were made at the same time over 18 months. Altogether, the movies cost $300 million. The risk was worth it. Tolkien fans loved the films, which made back many times their cost.

"The New Zealand director who masterminded this film has made a work for, and of, our times."
—Roger Ebert, *Chicago Sun-Times*

More important, the movies showed how amazing and realistic computer animation could be. This animation combined with dramatic landscapes and talented actors to set a new standard for fantasy films.

DID YOU KNOW?

We first meet Frodo Baggins at his uncle Bilbo's 111th birthday party. During filming, the 111 candles kept setting the cake on fire. The cake was made of plastic.

#7 Jaws

What is scarier than the monster you see? The monster you don't see! That simple idea made *Jaws* one of the most terrifying movies ever. Audiences didn't get a good look at the 25-foot (7.5-meter) great white shark until the end of the movie. Anyone who went to the movies in 1975 remembers *Jaws*. And anyone who went to the beach that summer remembers how hard it was to go in the water.

Roll Credits

Film: *Jaws*
Year: 1975
Studio: Universal
Director: Steven Spielberg
Stars: Robert Shaw (Quint), Roy Scheider (Chief Brody), Richard Dreyfuss (Matt Hooper), Lorraine Gary (Ellen Brody)
Oscar nominations: 4
Oscar wins: 3

Steven Spielberg's mechanical great white shark terrified movie audiences during the summer of 1975.

Big Problems

In the days before computer animation, there was only one way to make a movie starring a gigantic shark: You needed a gigantic shark. This is why director Steven Spielberg had three mechanical sharks built for *Jaws*. But they never worked properly. The first time Spielberg tried to shoot a scene with a mechanical shark, it sank! Crewmembers started calling the film "Flaws."

Spielberg was forced to cut the mechanical shark from a number of scenes. That decision actually helped the film. The suspense built as audiences waited to see the shark. When it finally appeared, viewers were terrified!

CLASSIC QUOTE

"You're gonna need a bigger boat."

—Chief Brody, after his first glimpse of the shark

The New Hitchcock

Jaws was a blockbuster hit from the opening weekend. No one could remember another movie that still scared people days and weeks after they saw it. Spielberg was called a genius. He was compared to the legendary suspense director Alfred Hitchcock.

In the 1970s, most movies opened in a handful of theaters. They then spread across the country. *Jaws* was one of the first to go into "wide release." It opened in hundreds of theaters on the same day. The film started the trend for huge summer blockbusters—a trend that continues to this day.

Robert Shaw, Roy Scheider, and Richard Dreyfuss (left to right) starred in *Jaws*.

FOR THE RECORD

One reason *Jaws* was so scary was its score. Whenever the shark got close, a tune of two alternating notes was heard: *da-dum, da-dum*. This simple tune has become a classic piece of suspense music. John Williams wrote the score for *Jaws*. He also wrote the music for other blockbusters such as *Star Wars* and *Raiders of the Lost Ark*.

The scene where the shark first attacks is unforgettable. Many people became so scared that they refused to go in the ocean.

Practically Perfect

Jaws inspired many moviemakers to make horror films about animals. Young moviemakers studied every scene to learn how to keep moviegoers on the edge of their seats. Despite bad weather, sinking boats, and a shark that never really worked, Spielberg ended up with an almost perfect movie.

In the end, *Jaws* also had some negative impacts. The movie was so frightening that beach traffic dropped sharply in 1975. Also, shark hunting increased. Even today, many people think twice before going in the water.

DID YOU KNOW?

The most terrifying scene in *Jaws* occurs when the character Matt Hooper explores a wrecked boat and finds one of the shark's victims. Spielberg paid $3,000 of his own money to add the scene after Universal Studios refused to pay for it.

#8 The Lion King

What happens when you build a world-class team of animators, actors, screenwriters, and songwriters? You get a world-class blockbuster. It took six years for *The Lion King* to go from the drawing board to the silver screen. It was worth the wait. The tale of a young lion's rise to power was unforgettable, and it gave the world a new expression: "Hakuna Matata" ("No Worries").

Roll Credits

Film: *The Lion King*
Year: 1994
Studio: Walt Disney Studios
Directors: Roger Allers and Rob Minkoff
Stars: Jonathan Taylor Thomas and Matthew Broderick (Simba), Nathan Lane (Timon), Ernie Sabella (Pumbaa), Jeremy Irons (Scar), James Earl Jones (King Mufasa), Robert Guillaume (Rafiki)
Oscar nominations: 4
Oscar wins: 2

More than 1 million drawings were used in the making of *The Lion King*. The final version has almost 120,000 hand-colored frames.

African Adventure

In 1988, Disney animators began talking about a new movie set in Africa. It would be a challenge to create the landscape and its large groups of animals. To bring this world to life, they would need to combine hand-drawn animation with computer technology. In 1992, the script for *The Lion King* was ready, and the animation began. More than 600 people worked on the movie.

The animators studied film of live African animals. Several times, lions were brought to the studio. The artists learned how lions greet each other and how lions fight. A group of animators even went to Africa to learn how to draw the landscape correctly.

CLASSIC QUOTE

"Remember who you are. You are my son, and the one true king. Remember ..."

—Mufasa, talking to his cub Simba from beyond

Solid Start

Walt Disney Studios worked on *The Lion King* and *Pocahontas* at the same time. Several artists thought *Pocahontas* would be more popular. They asked to be switched to that movie. Both films did well, but *The Lion King* "won." It made more than $780 million around the world.

Critics loved *The Lion King*. They were amazed by the animation and charmed by the songs. They also liked how Simba grew from a frightened cub to a courageous king.

After the lion cub Simba is born, he is held up for all the animals to see.

FOR THE RECORD

Rock star Elton John was asked to write the songs for *The Lion King*. He wasn't satisfied with the songs he and Tim Rice wrote for the movie. But audiences loved them. His songs are now considered high points of the movie. "Can You Feel the Love Tonight," "Hakuna Matata," and "Circle of Life" all received Academy Award nominations for best original song. "Can You Feel the Love Tonight" won the award.

Simba, Timon, and Pumbaa form a special friendship in *The Lion King*.

Disney Comeback

From the 1930s to the 1960s, Disney made many classic animated movies. These include *Snow White and the Seven Dwarfs*, *Bambi*, and *Sleeping Beauty*. In the 1970s and 1980s, its movies were not big hits. Then, in 1989, Disney made *The Little Mermaid.* The hit film started a great Disney comeback. Films such as *The Lion King, Beauty and the Beast,* and *Aladdin* helped Disney regain its place in the world of animation.

In 1997, *The Lion King* was made into a musical that opened on Broadway. The play's giant puppets wowed audiences, and it went on to become one of the longest-running shows on Broadway.

DID YOU KNOW?

Characters from *The Lion King* show up in two other Disney movies—*Hercules* and *Aladdin and the King of Thieves*. The song "Hakuna Matata" plays on a car radio at the end of *Toy Story*.

Spider-Man

Turning comic books into movies isn't always easy. The movie has to meet the expectations of comic book fans and other moviegoers. The makers of *Spider-Man* transformed the superhero's story into a box-office smash. They found the right mix of special effects and good acting. Peter Parker was a character that people liked and understood. His romance with Mary Jane Watson was touching. That made *Spider-Man* a huge hit when he swung into movie theaters across America.

ROLL CREDITS

Film: *Spider-Man*
Year: 2002
Studio: Columbia Pictures
Director: Sam Raimi
Stars: Tobey Maguire (Peter Parker/Spider-Man), Willem Dafoe (Norman Osborn/Green Goblin), James Franco (Harry Osborn), Kirsten Dunst (Mary Jane Watson), Rosemary Harris (May Parker), Cliff Robertson (Ben Parker)
Oscar nominations: 2 **Oscar wins:** 0

Long Time Coming

Spider-Man has been a popular superhero since he was created by Marvel Comics in 1962. Movie studios had been trying to bring Spider-Man to the big screen since the early 1980s. But no one could figure out the best way to bring him to life. Finally, in 2001, filming started. Columbia Pictures had the right script, the right director, and the right star in Tobey Maguire. The filmmakers thought he was the best choice to play Peter Parker, an average teenager who gains superpowers.

CLASSIC QUOTE

"You know who I am. ... Your friendly neighborhood Spider-Man."

—Spider-Man

Even more important, CGI was available. Spider-Man needed to be able to shoot webs from his wrists. He needed to be able to climb walls. For some scenes, the moviemakers filmed Maguire wearing the Spider-Man suit. In many other scenes, Spider-Man is a complete CGI creation.

Audiences loved seeing Spider-Man save the day.

Solid Start

Spider-Man premiered in the spring of 2002. Audiences loved it. Fans of "Spidey" were thrilled. They said the film was faithful to the comic book. It was true to how Peter Parker became Spider-Man, began fighting crime, and battled the Green Goblin.

Spider-Man set U.S. records for the most money made in its first weekend and in a single day. In the end, *Spider-Man* made $821 million worldwide. No movie made more money that year.

Spider-Man does whatever it takes to keep Mary Jane safe from harm.

FOR THE RECORD

Spider-Man was created by Stan Lee, who began writing comic books when he was 18 years old. By the 1960s, Lee had helped create many classic characters, including the Incredible Hulk, Iron Man, the X-Men, and, of course, Spider-Man. For years, most superheroes were almost perfect people. Lee's characters had more flaws and were more human. They got angry, worried, and sick. Lee's innovations made Marvel Comics into a comic book powerhouse, and they made Lee into a legend.

Super Movie

The success of *Spider-Man* had a big effect on the movie business. It became one of the top 20 moneymakers of all time. Studios that had been afraid of films based on comic books now started making them. Meanwhile, Columbia Pictures made two popular sequels, *Spider-Man II* and *Spider-Man III*.

When *Spider-Man* was released in 2002, it made more money than any superhero movie in history. In 2008, *The Dark Knight* passed it. Like *Spider-Man*, this Batman movie was true to its comic-book roots.

Spider-Man **kicked off a new wave of movies based on comic books.**

DID YOU KNOW?

When Peter Parker first tries to shoot his web, he says "Shazam!" and "Up, up, and away!" These are famous lines from superheroes Captain Marvel and Superman.

Finding Nemo

Could a movie about fish make people laugh? Could it also make them cry? That is what audiences wondered as they settled into their seats to watch *Finding Nemo*. What they saw was a beautifully animated story with heart and humor. *Finding Nemo* became more than a hit. By the time it left theaters, the movie swam to the top of the box office as the biggest G-rated movie in history.

Roll Credits

Film: *Finding Nemo*
Year: 2003
Studios: Pixar and Walt Disney studios
Director: Andrew Stanton
Stars: Albert Brooks (Marlin), Alexander Gould (Nemo), Ellen DeGeneres (Dory), Willem Dafoe (Gill), Geoffrey Rush (Nigel), Brad Garrett (Bloat)
Oscar nominations: 4
Oscar wins: 1

Dory (top) becomes friends with Marlin and helps him find Nemo.

Father and Son

In 1997, Andrew Stanton of Pixar Studios began planning a story about a fish named Nemo. Stanton had written the studio's first big hit, *Toy Story*. Three years later, a team of 180 people at Pixar began making *Finding Nemo.* The film tells the story of an overprotective clown fish father named Marlin. Marlin searches for his son, Nemo, who was captured and put in a fish tank in a dentist's office in Australia.

To learn more about fish, several Pixar animators went scuba diving in California, Hawaii, and Australia. They also met with scientists who study fish. The scientists explained how fish move and behave.

CLASSIC QUOTE

"I wanna go home. Does anyone know where my dad is?"

—Nemo

***Finding Nemo* is action-packed, funny, and touching—all at the same time.**

Record Breaker

After the success of *Toy Story* and other Pixar films, the pressure was on Stanton and the his crew to deliver another hit. They didn't have to worry. Audiences fell in love with *Finding Nemo*. The movie became Pixar's biggest hit yet. It eventually took in $864 million worldwide. That made it the top animated movie of all time.

The DVD of *Finding Nemo* went on sale November 4, 2003. More than 6 million copies were sold that day. *Finding Nemo* has become the best-selling DVD in history.

FOR THE RECORD

For decades, animated feature films were drawn only by hand. By the early 1990s, animators were mixing hand-drawn images with CGI. Then, in 1995, Pixar changed animated movies forever by producing *Toy Story*. It was the first all-CGI feature film. In the years that followed, Pixar produced the hits *A Bug's Life*, *Toy Story 2*, and *Monsters, Inc.*, before making the blockbuster *Finding Nemo*.

Woody and Buzz Lightyear are talkative toys in *Toy Story*.

In *Finding Nemo*, computer animation brought the undersea world to life.

Computer Games

Finding Nemo won the Oscar for best animated feature. In later Pixar films, such as *The Incredibles* and *Wall-E*, the animation was even better. The characters looked even more realistic.

"It adds an unexpected beauty, a use of color and form that makes it one of those rare movies where I wanted to sit in the front row."

—Roger Ebert, *Chicago Sun-Times*

Thanks to films like *Finding Nemo*, it may someday be impossible to tell the difference between a live clown fish and an animated one … until the animated fish starts talking!

DID YOU KNOW?

After *Finding Nemo*, pet stores saw a sharp rise in the sale of clown fish and saltwater aquariums. Tourism in Australia increased, too. Many people visited to see clown fish. Everyone wanted to "find Nemo."

Honorable Mentions

Raiders of the Lost Ark (1981)

In 1977, superstar directors George Lucas and Steven Spielberg decided to make an old-time action-adventure movie together. At first, every major Hollywood studio rejected their idea! Paramount finally agreed to do the picture. *Raiders of the Lost Ark* was the most popular movie of 1981. It made more than $380 million by the time it left the theaters. Three other Indiana Jones movies followed. *Indiana Jones and the Kingdom of the Crystal Skull* was released in 2008. More than 25 years after the original film, Harrison Ford was still going strong as Indiana Jones.

Pirates of the Caribbean: The Curse of the Black Pearl (2003)

For years, one of the most popular rides in the Disney theme parks was Pirates of the Caribbean. When Disney announced that it was making a movie with the same name, many people thought it would fail. But *Pirates of the Caribbean: The Curse of the Black Pearl* was a smash hit. The creativity of the actors and the amazing computer effects helped the film make more than $650 million. The film was followed by two hit sequels.

Glossary

Academy Awards: awards given each year to members of the movie industry. Several people are nominated in each category. The winner receives a golden statue called an Oscar.

animators: artists who work to make cartoons appear to be alive

budget: the amount of money available to make a specific movie

computer-generated imagery (CGI): technology that involves using computers to make the animation or special visual effects for movies.

critics: people who write reviews of movies, TV shows, music, and other forms of art

cinematography: the art of filming a movie

footage: a section of film from a movie

premiered: shown in public for the first time

producer: a person who supervises the making of a movie, music recording, or TV show

rights: the permission to make a story into a movie

score: the music for a movie

sequel: a movie that continues the story of an earlier movie or has the same characters

soundtrack: a recording of the music used in a movie

For More Information

Books

Burr, Ty. *The Best Old Movies for Families: A Guide to Watching Together.* New York: Anchor Books, 2007.

Horn, Geoffrey M. *Movie Acting* (Making Movies). Pleasantville, NY: Gareth Stevens, 2006.

Lekich, John. *Reel Adventures: The Savvy Teens' Guide to Great Movies.* Toronto: Annick Press, 2002.

Simpson, Paul. *The Rough Guide to Kids' Movies.* London: Rough Guides, 2004.

Web Sites

Academy Awards Database
http://awardsdatabase.oscars.org
Go to this site to find out who was nominated and who won every Oscar in history.

Yahoo! Kids: Movies
http://kids.yahoo.com/movies
This guide provides the latest movie news and film clips.

Index

About the Author

Mark Stewart has written more than 200 nonfiction books for schools and libraries. He does not claim to be the "ultimate" movie author, but he did once star in a movie. Mark played Zachary Zween in the 1971 film *The Story of Zachary Zween.* It was based on a book of the same name by Mabel Watts. The movie was not a blockbuster, but Mark's daughters get a kick out of watching it today.